This is a clip art book!

What is clip art? In our case, it's hundreds of drawings, charts, forms, and stories that a youth worker can clip out and glue together into a nearly infinite array of attractive and exciting mail outs, posters, greeting cards, overhead transparencies and the like. Most of all, it's FUN!

Even better, it saves a ton of work! Why spend hours trying to draw a snow scene for your winter camp announcement when we have several great snow scenes in the "Clip Art" chapter? Why spill ink all over your mail out when we've already spilled it for you in the "Backgrounds" section?

Yes, indeed, you'll find the **YOUTH WORKER'S CLIP ART BOOK** to be one of the best investments you have ever made. We hope you enjoy it.

ISBN: 0-8307-1014-0

INTERNATIONAL CENTER FOR LEARNING

THE YOUTH WORKER'S **CLIP ART BOOK**

Everything you need for a year's worth of mail outs, and more.

CONTENTS
Each section listed below contains complete instructions and illustrations to guide you along.

MAIL OUTS MADE EASY
How to use clip art to make fantastic mail outs, posters, Bible study worksheets, greeting cards and more.

CLIP ART SECTION
All the art you need to put together a ton of great stuff. Featuring the best art from four Christian cartoonists.

BACKGROUNDS
Wild and wacky backgrounds to give your mail outs some snap.

STATIONERY
Great looking stationery for the youth worker who has everything, and wants to put it in the mail.

GREETING CARDS
Birthday, get well, thank you, and "We miss you" cards. Postcards and graduation cards, too.

FORMS
Medical release forms, journals, prayer charts, calendars, comment cards, and a bunch more very useful forms.

SPIRITUAL VITAMINS
Short stories you can include in your mail outs. Enough for a year's worth of monthlies.

MISCELLANEOUS CERTIFICATES, AWARDS AND SO ON
Attendance awards, admission tickets, etc.

HOW TO SURVIVE THE PRINTERS
A helpful look at how to get your beautiful stuff printed without going crazy. A list of services a small print shop can offer you and a glossary of artist's and printer's terms.

TIPS ON PHOTOCOPYING
Some things to keep in mind.

MAIL OUTS MADE EASY

YOU CAN DO IT!

Just follow the step-by-step instructions in this book and we guarantee that you'll turn out some real eye-poppin' pieces of artwork.

Here's how . . .

PART ONE: THE TOOLS AND SUPPLIES YOU'LL NEED

You can buy these tools and supplies at art supply stores, stationery stores and most department stores.

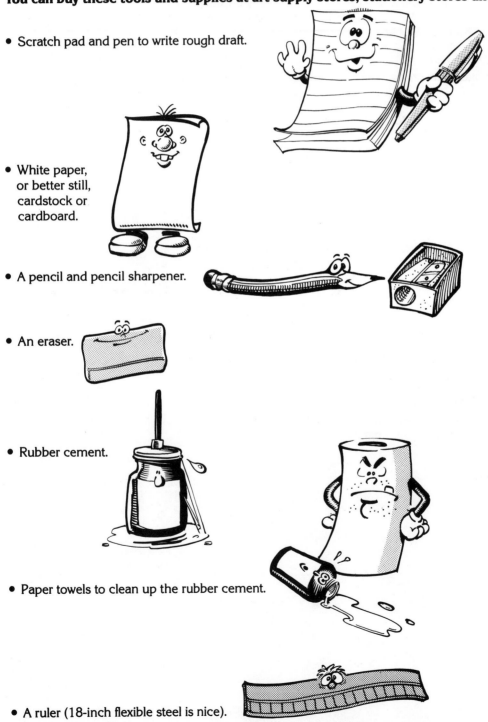

- Scratch pad and pen to write rough draft.

- White paper, or better still, cardstock or cardboard.

- A pencil and pencil sharpener.

- An eraser.

- Rubber cement.

- Paper towels to clean up the rubber cement.

- A ruler (18-inch flexible steel is nice).

- A 45° triangle, to help lay out guidelines. Get a clear plastic one so you can see through it as you draw lines.

- Three felt pens (fine, medium, and wide point for handlettering).

- A bottle of Liquid Paper correction fluid, for when you mess up.

- Scissors.

- And, of course, this book.

Optional tools:

- An X-Acto knife or equivalent. Make sure you buy #11 blades which are shaped like this:

The most comfortable knives to work with are shaped like fountain pens.

- Speedball brand nibs and handles, for making better looking letters than the felt pens. We recommend that you get Speedball nibs B-6 (fine line), B-5½, B-5 (mediums) and one or two big fat ones for headlines. Buy a handle for each one.

- You'll need ink for your pens. Black Magic brand ink (don't worry, it's not demonic!) is probably the best. If you intend to use a lot of ink, buy a large refill bottle. It's much cheaper that way.

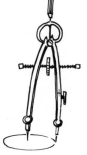

- A compass for drawing circles.

- An electric sharpener or manual pencil pointer.

- Technical pens. Technical drawing pens are expensive little toys and can be a pain to clean. But they can be very useful. Ask at your art store for Mars, Rapid-O-Graph and other brands.

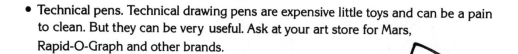

- A drawing table and drawing lamp. Much better than the back strain and eyestrain you'll get at your desk!

Literally thousands of different rub-on type styles (alphabets and numbers) and rub-on backgrounds (dots, stripes, etc.) are available on large sheets. Here are some examples:

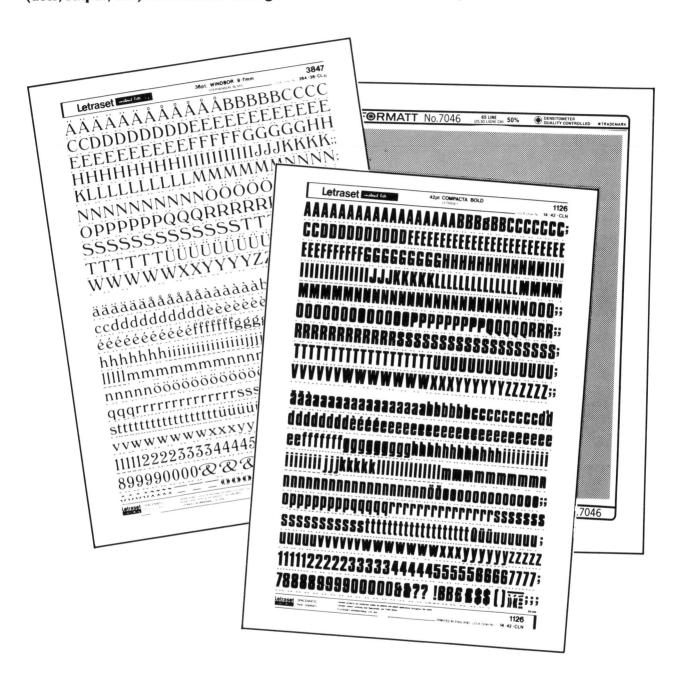

Ask to see a manufacturer's catalog at your art store. You'll be amazed at what you can buy. Rub-on or peel and stick letters take a long time to apply, but they really make your mail outs look professional.

Store in plastic envelopes or the letters will chip and crack.

PART TWO: THE TECHNIQUE

Here's the simple way to turn a blank sheet of paper into a masterpiece . . .

The basic formula:

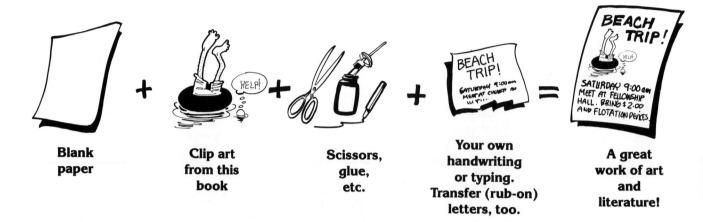

Blank paper + **Clip art from this book** + **Scissors, glue, etc.** + **Your own handwriting or typing. Transfer (rub-on) letters, too.** = **A great work of art and literature!**

OK! Ready to have some fun? Let's go . . .

STEP ONE: Decide what you want your mail out to be about. Let's say it's a trip to snow camp. Write a rough draft.

STEP TWO: Decide what the format of your printed product will be. By that we mean, will it be on 8½″ × 11″ paper? Maybe 11″ × 17″? Or, even an odd size which would require trimming from a standard size when printed.

Some small print shops can't handle 11″ × 17″ paper, so be sure to find out.

STEP THREE: Cut a "paste-up sheet" the same size as the final product. This is the sheet of paper to which you'll glue the artwork, draw the lettering, and deliver to the printer. Always handle with care and don't get smudgy fingerprints on it! We suggest heavy cardstock. It's easy to cut to size and more durable than paper.

You can also use graph paper, the kind with light blue lines. The lines will keep your art and lettering nice and straight, and the light blue ink does not reproduce on photocopiers or printing presses. Buy good quality graph paper so that the ink you use won't bleed and turn fuzzy.

STEP FOUR: Find the appropriate pieces of artwork in this book. For example:

Cut the artwork out of this book. You'll notice that each page is perforated for easy removal. Most of the artwork has been reproduced in more than one size to give you flexibility in page design.

STEP FIVE: Now you must determine where to position the art and copy. Either make a few pencil sketches on scrap paper, or decide in your mind the basic arrangement you will use.

STEP SIX: Use rubber cement (follow the manufacturer's directions) to glue the artwork to the paste-up sheet. Rubber cement is not permanent, so handle your paste-up gently. We like rubber cement because it's so easy to clean up. Incidentally, leave a ½" or better margin on your paper, unless you intend to "bleed" your art (see glossary in "HOW TO SURVIVE THE PRINTERS" section.

STEP SEVEN: Use a pencil and triangle to draw light guidelines for lettering. Or use graph paper.

STEP EIGHT: Letter everything with felt pens or pen and ink, or type your copy on paper. Then cut it out and paste it up. You can also use transfer letters as mentioned before. The manufacturer supplies instructions either with the letters or in the manufacturer's catalog.

A HELPFUL HINT: You can avoid the frustration of wrecking your paste-up with lettering mistakes by lettering on a separate piece of paper. Glue that paper to your paste-up.

STEP NINE: After everything is good and dry, correct all errors and erase all pencil lines. There you have it!

STEP TEN: You're ready for the print shop. Turn to "HOW TO SURVIVE THE PRINTERS" section for tips on getting your stuff printed. Or, if you intend to photocopy your project, read "TIPS ON PHOTOCOPYING."

CLIP ART SECTION

The following pages contain more than enough artwork for a year's worth of junior and senior high youth program events. The artwork has been printed on only one side of each page so that you may cut it out without ruining something on the back.

We hope you find a ton of uses for this section! Use your imagination, or better still, get somebody else to do this for you and make them use their imaginations!

Here is a list of just some of the subjects covered:

Winter camp
Summer camp
Water skiing
Snow skiing
Roller skating parties
Beach parties
Pool parties
Ice cream socials
Barbecues
River rafting trips
Slumber parties
Christmas parties
Halloween parties
Thanksgiving parties
Miniature golf
Valentine parties
Hayrides
The bus (for bus route info.)
Fireworks parties
Slave contests
Dye wars
Zoo trips
Movie night
Campouts and backpacking
Concerts
Bike hikes
Amusement park trips
Mud Bowl games
Car and bike rallies
Scavenger hunt
School's out party
New Year's party
Sex talks
Picnics
Canoe trips
Rock climbing
Ice skating
Water slide
Game night
Lots of Bible meeting stuff
And more!

P.S. By using an opaque projector, you can make giant posters.

SUMMER CAMP

SUMMER CAMP

SUMMER CAMP!

SUMMER CAMP!

GOD'S WORD

SUMMER CAMP!

GOD'S WORD

Winter Camp!

Winter Camp!

Games for dirtballs

Squirt guns, dye wars

Capture the flag games

HAY-RIDE!

HAY-RIDE!

HAY-RIDE!

Water balloons

BONK

MINIATURE GOLF

Amusement parks

Bike hikes, bike rallies

Car rally
(Oops! Wrong kind of rally!)

Rock climbing

Roller-skate parties

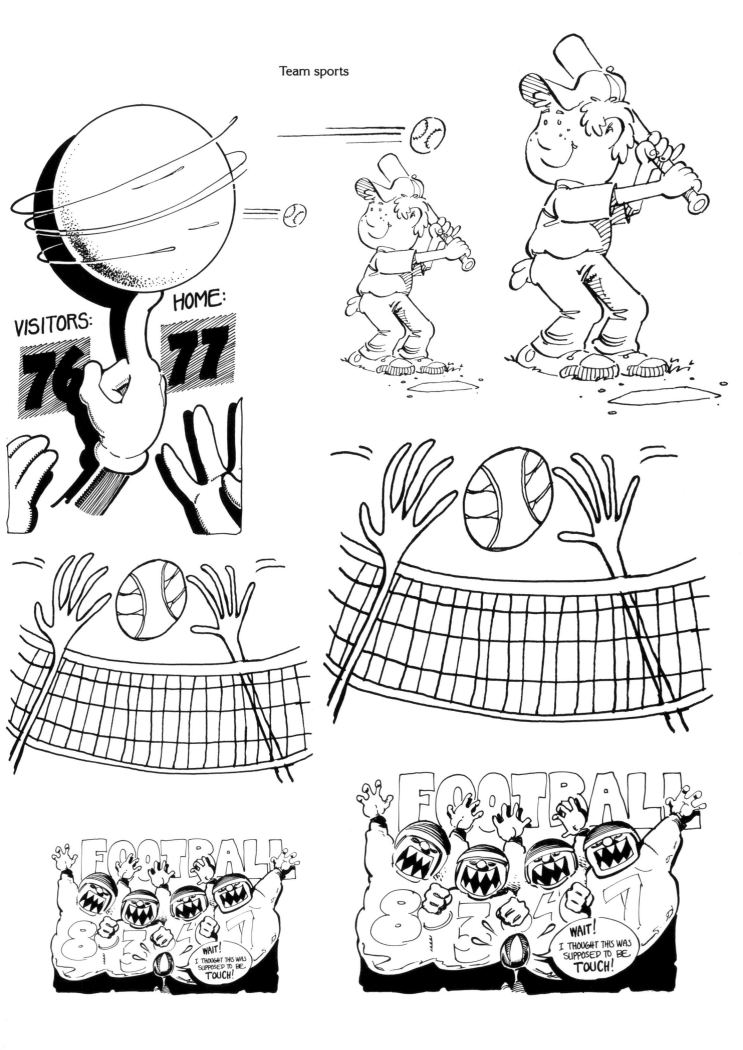

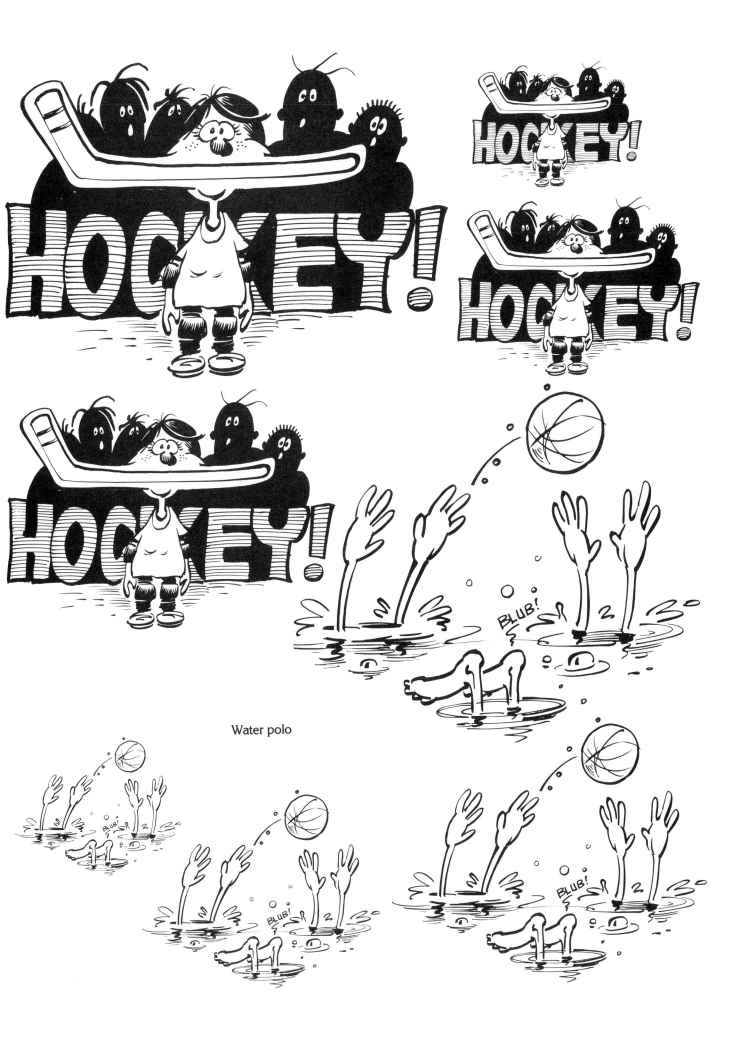

Water polo

Concerts and choirs

Typical game night games

Chariot races

Slave contests

Slumber parties

Movie parties

Christmas parties

Christ
the Savior
is
born—

Christ
the Savior
is
born—

Merry Christmas!

Merry Christmas!

Merry Christmas

New Year's Eve parties

Valentine's Day

Easter

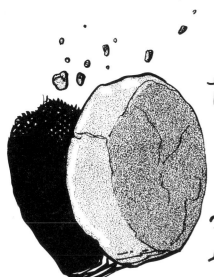

the stone was rolled away.

"He is Risen"

the stone was rolled away.

"He is Risen"

the stone was
rolled away.

"He is
Risen".

CHRIST'S
LOVE

CHRIST'S
LOVE

Summer vacation parties

Summer is over parties

Halloween parties

Thanksgiving

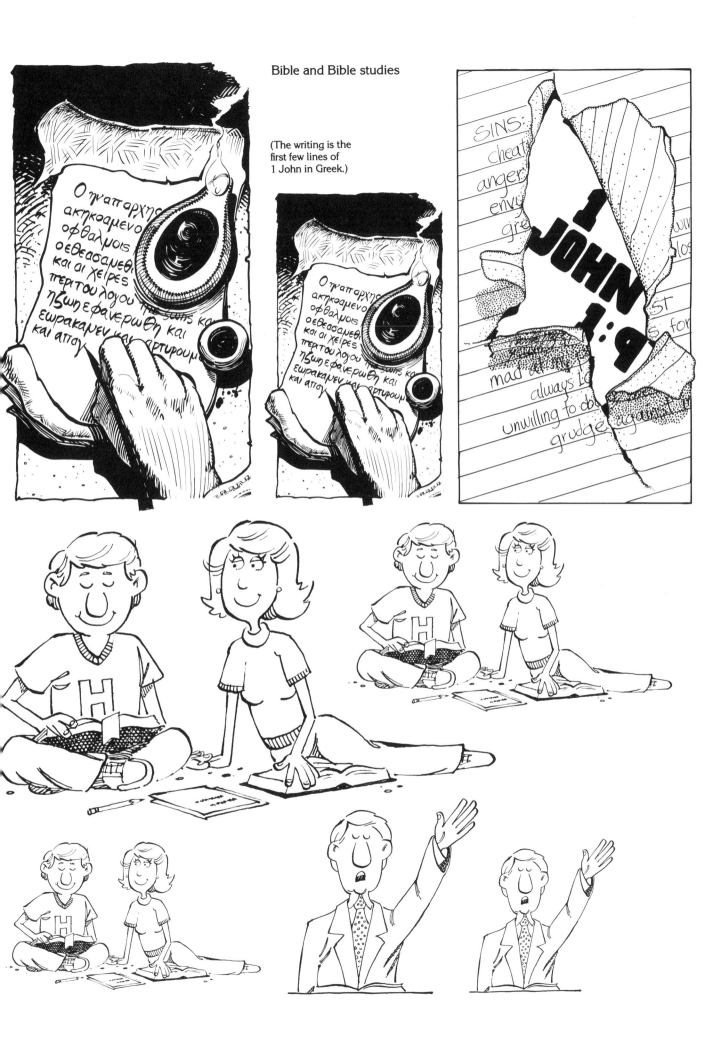

Bible and Bible studies

(The writing is the first few lines of 1 John in Greek.)

The Lord's Supper

The Lord's Supper

JESUS!

GOD'S SON, SAVIOR!

JESUS!

GOD'S SON, SAVIOR!

The shackles broken

"The truth shall make you free."

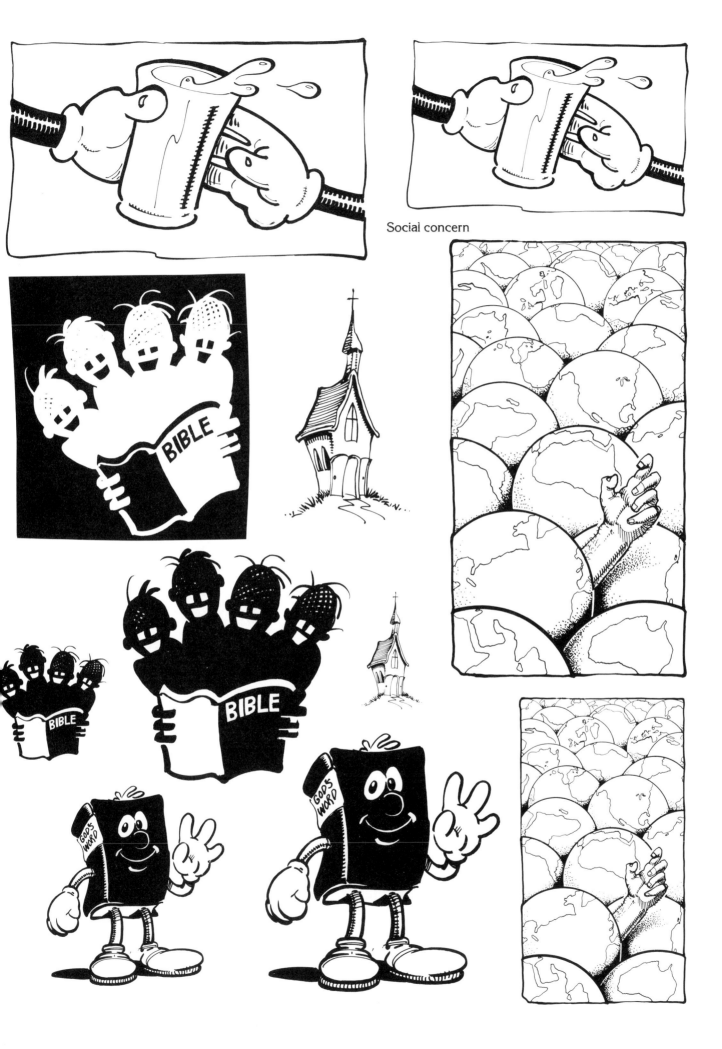

Social concern

"What time is that meeting?"

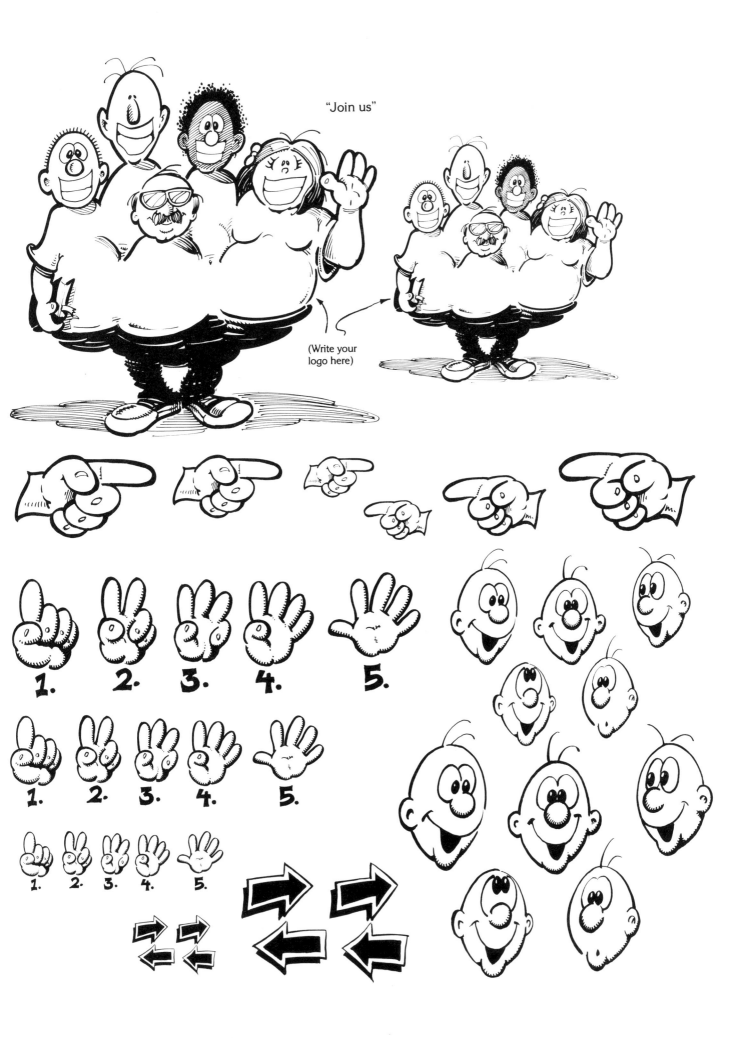

BACKGROUNDS

If you really want to spice up your mail outs, try using some of these wild and wacky backgrounds. Suggestions:

IMPORTANT NOTE: The size of each background page, after it has been detached from this book, is only 8″ × 11″. Therefore, in order to completely fill an 8½″ × 11″ piece of paper, your final paste-up must be enlarged. This is easy to do. Simply tell the printer to enlarge the paste-up to fit. (This requires a 106% enlargement.)

If you intend to reproduce your paste-up on a photocopy machine which does not enlarge, you can trim the excess from the final copies.

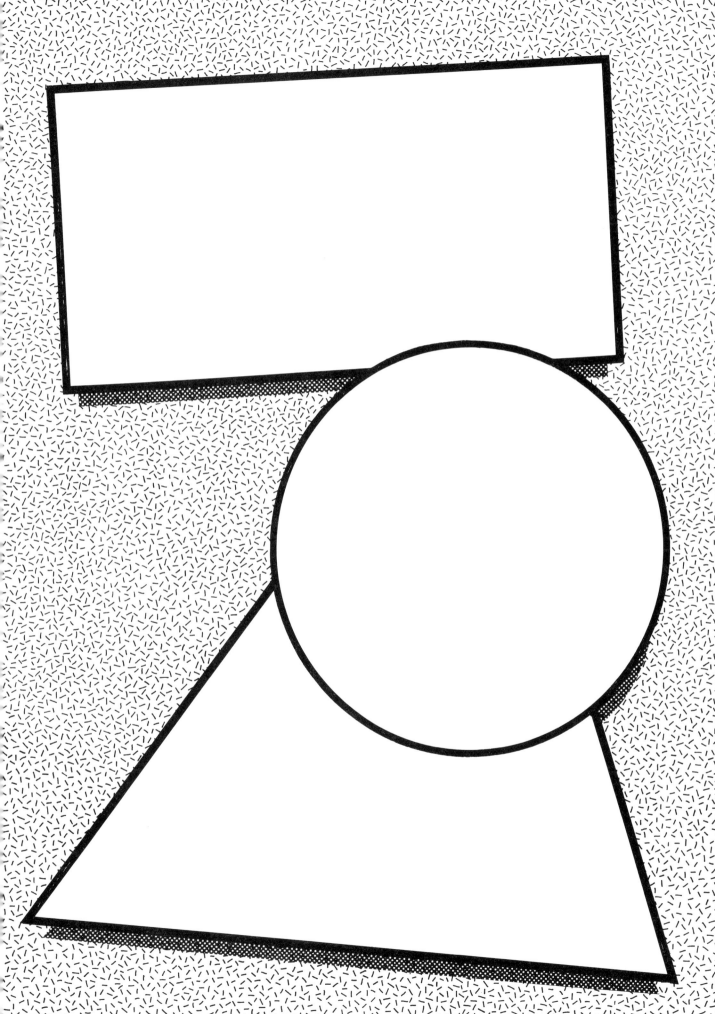

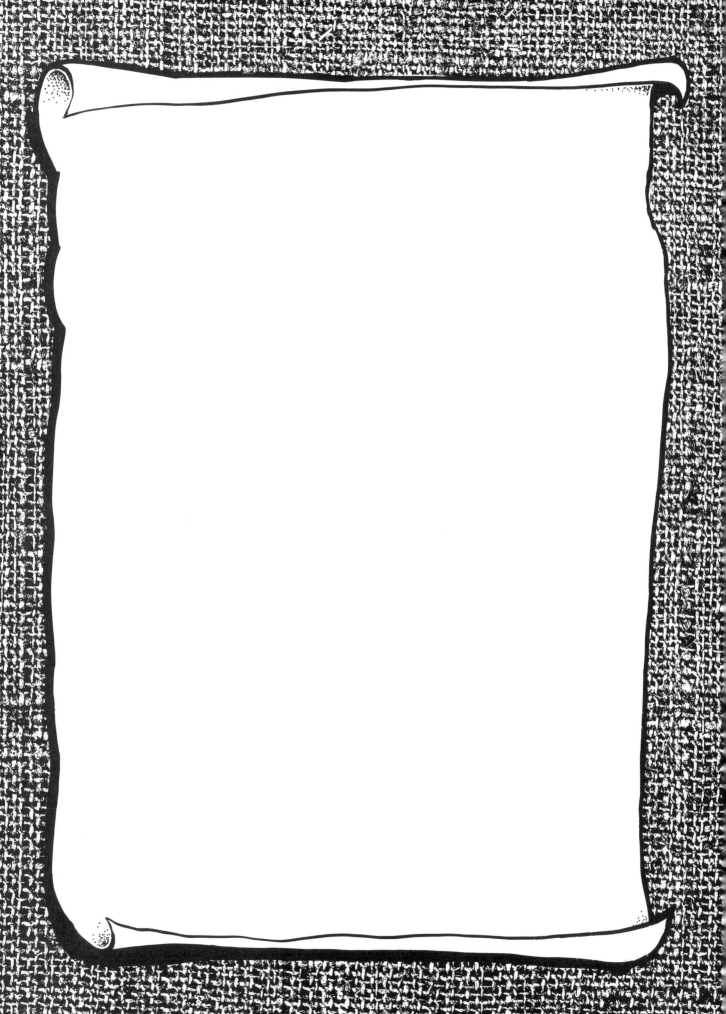

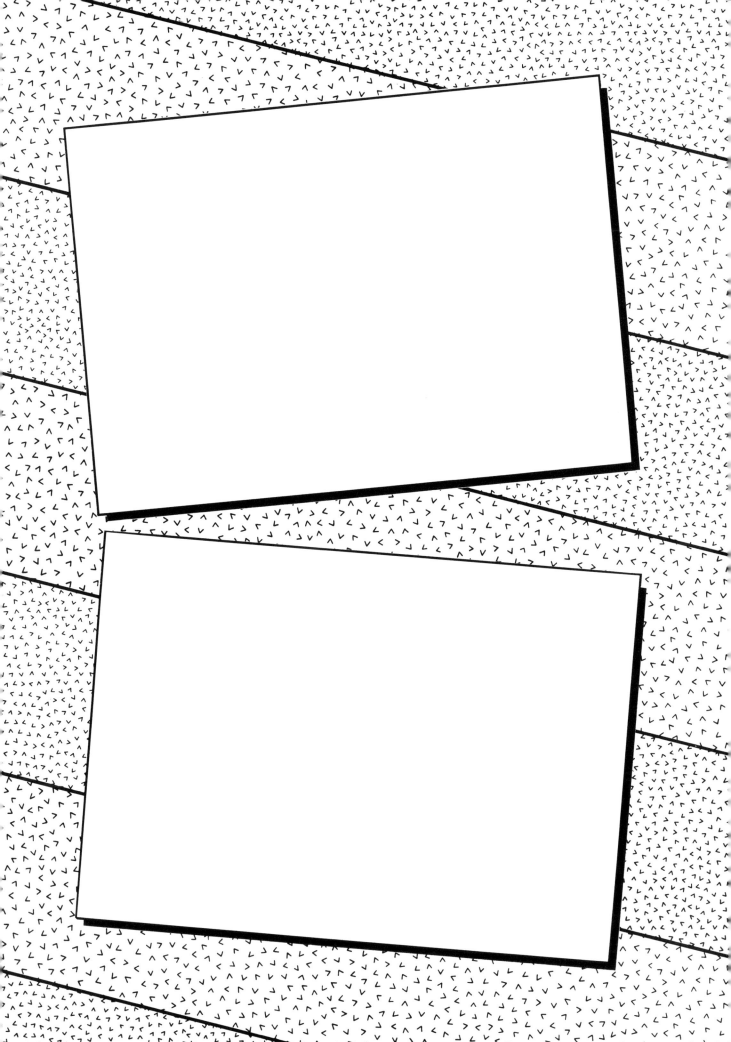

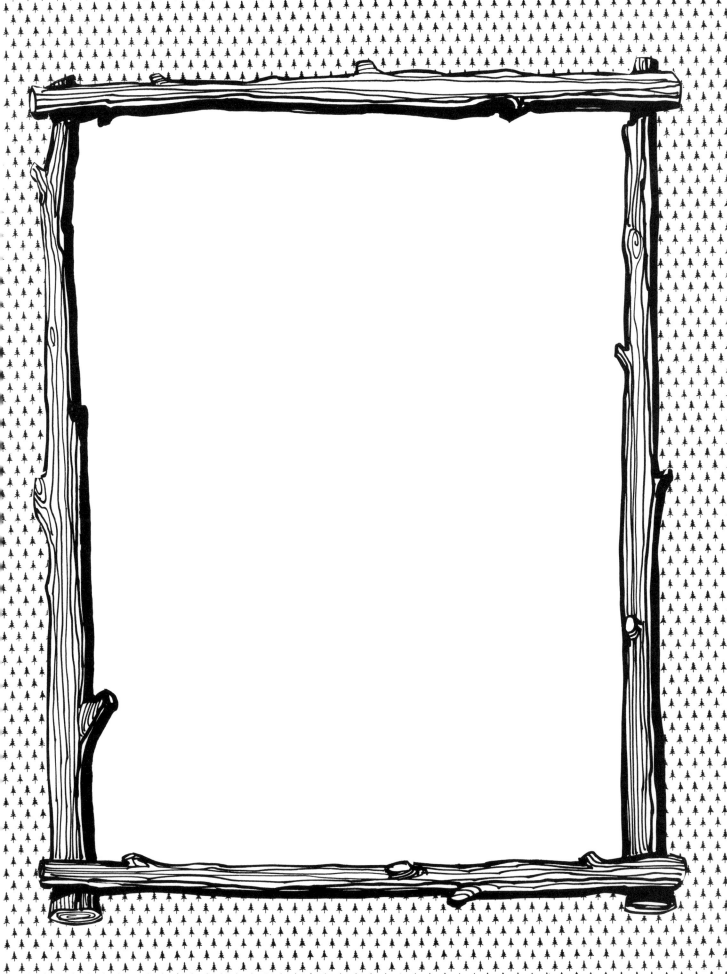

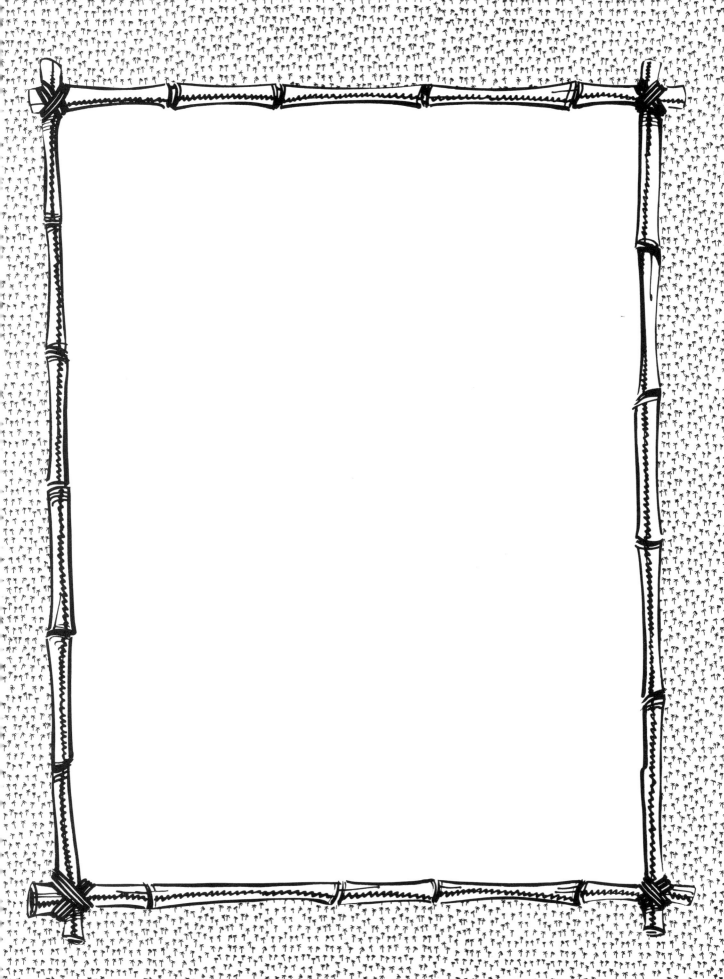

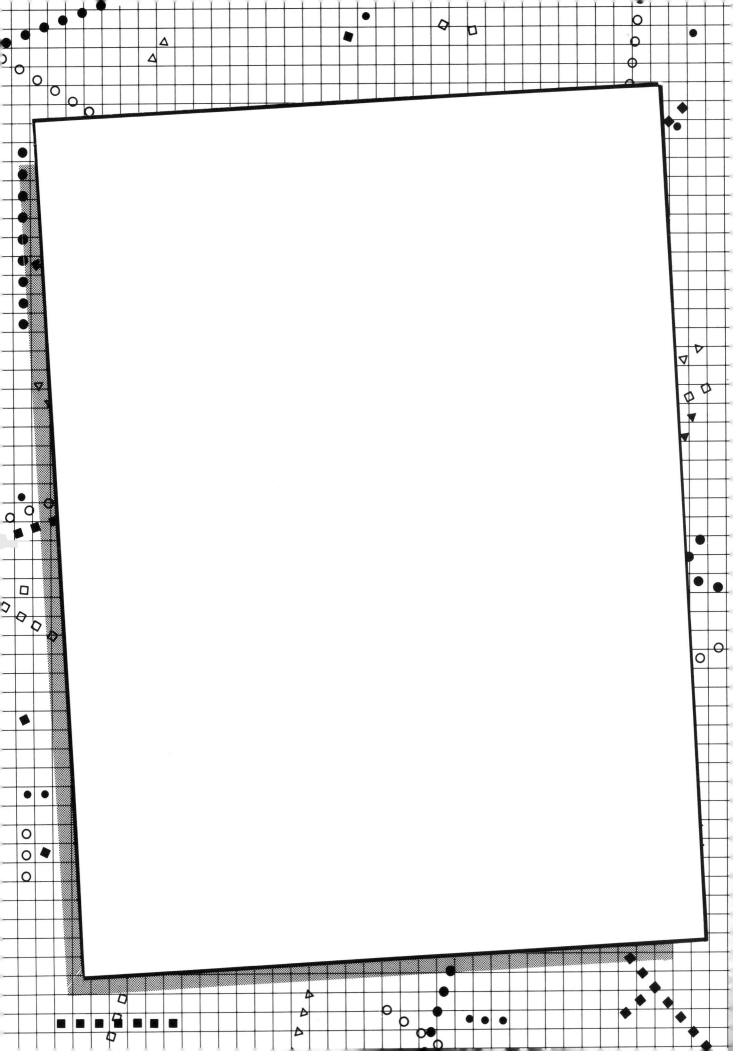

STATIONERY

As long as you're going to the expense of sending a mail out to the millions of kids in your youth group, you may as well stuff those envelopes as full as they can get. Why not print up your own special stationery? Be sure to put your office and/or home address and phone number and all the other things people put on stationery. We recommend that you compose a letter pointing out all the great activities on the enclosed mail out. Add any special notes and throw in a short story from our "Spiritual Vitamins" chapter. Once printed, take time to handwrite short notes to a few of the kids. They'll love you for it.

NOTE: Unlike the pages in the "BACKGROUNDS" section, these pages do not require enlargement. Of course, the background pages would also make great stationery.

 Just a note....

GREETING CARDS

Kids love to get mail. Remember how you used to read the junk addressed to "Occupant"? It's special when a kid receives a personal note or thought from you. That's why we designed these great greeting cards.

- **Three different birthday cards**
- **Two different get well cards**
- **Two "We miss you" cards**
- **Two graduation cards**
- **A thank you card to give to your youth group sponsors.**

The pages containing all the cards have been mocked-up on this page and the next. They are numbered in order of appearance and sides A and B of each card is indicated (side A is the front of the card, side B is the inside). There is no side B for page 7.

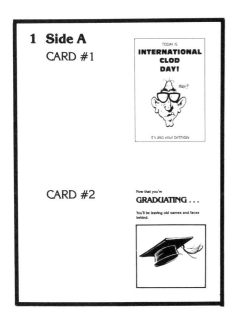

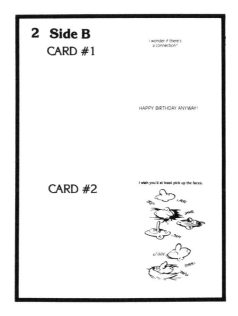

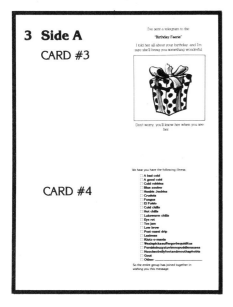

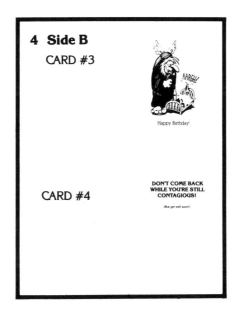

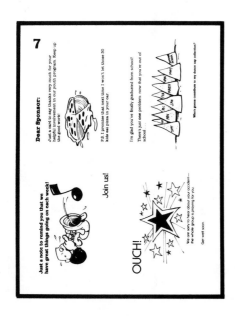

When these cards are printed, sides A and B are printed on opposite sides of the page. Be sure to identify, for the printer's benefit, which page goes where. See our instructions in "HOW TO SURVIVE THE PRINTERS."

These cards are all designed to fit two or four at a time on an 8½" × 11" piece of paper. Cut the printed cards apart and you get two or four for the price of one!

You should plan on printing these cards on heavy paper or cardstock. Call your printer for price quotes. Don't forget to insert your church or youth group's name where necessary.

After your cards are printed, cut and fold as shown.
Your printer can do this for you.

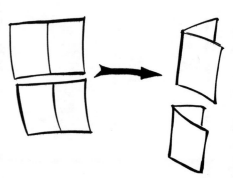

TODAY IS

INTERNATIONAL CLOD DAY!

HUH?

It's also your birthday . . .

Now that you're

GRADUATING . . .

You'll be leaving old names and faces behind.

I wonder if there's
a connection?

HAPPY BIRTHDAY ANYWAY!

I wish you'd at least pick up the faces.

I've sent a telegram to the

"Birthday Faerie"

I told her all about your birthday, and I'm sure she'll bring you something wonderful.

Don't worry, you'll know her when you see her . . .

We hear you have the following illness:

☐ **A bad cold**
☐ **A good cold**
☐ **Cold robbies**
☐ **Blue zoober**
☐ **Heebie Jeebies**
☐ **Crudola**
☐ **Fungus**
☐ **El Foldo**
☐ **Cold chills**
☐ **Hot chills**
☐ **Lukewarm chills**
☐ **Eye rot**
☐ **Toe jam**
☐ **Low brow**
☐ **Post-nasel drip**
☐ **Laziness**
☐ **Klutz-o-mania**
☐ **Wexlepickasuffergorbsquiditus**
☐ **Fernblobuxyztuvlmnopuddlenausea**
☐ **Hoochsobellyfootandmouthaphobia**
☐ **Gout**
☐ **Other:** _____

So the entire group has joined together in wishing you this message:

Happy Birthday!

**DON'T COME BACK
WHILE YOU'RE STILL
CONTAGIOUS!**

(But get well soon!)

I've got this overwhelming urge to give you all my **money** for your **birthday!**

I feel compelled to send you every dollar!

I can't resist! It must be some kind of **SICKNESS!**

And so . . .

Our records indicate that it's been

☐ 3 months
☐ 6 months
☐ 12 months

since your last dentist appointment . . .

Oops—I just got better.

Happy Birthday!

Not only that, but we haven't seen
you around here lately, either!
WE MISS YOU!

(P.S. If you let us drill your teeth, we'll give
you a free balloon.)

Dear Sponsor:

Just a card to say thanks very much for your helpful involvement in our youth program. Keep up the good work!

P.S. I promise that next time I won't let those 30 kids eat pizza in your car.

I'm glad you've finally graduated from school!

There's just **one** problem: now that you're out of school . . .

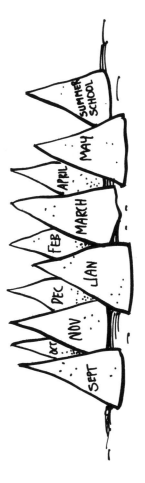

Who's gonna contribute to my dunce cap collection?

Just a note to remind you that we have great things going on each week!

Join us!

OUCH!

We are sorry to hear about your accident— the whole group is praying for you.

Get well soon.

FORMS

This section will save you a whole lot of typing! We've got every form and chart a youth worker could ever need! Well, maybe not EVERY one, but almost.

Tear out the forms you want. Take them to your print shop or have them copied on your office photocopier.

If you get in the habit of using these forms to keep your important records—some are for your youth group members to use—you'll find that you are much more organized and that you'll be able to deal with, say, the treasurer when he or she screams, "How could you spend $200.00 taking three kids to the beach!?!"

HERE'S WHAT YOU'LL FIND IN THIS SECTION:

- Two "journal" pages. One to keep important notes about each and every one of your special events and activities. The other for regular meetings. We strongly urge you to keep records. A year or two down the road you'll be glad you did!

REGULARLY SCHEDULED MEETING JOURNAL

Name of meeting __WED. NITE BIBLE STUDY__

DATE	SUBJECT OR GUEST	ATTENDANCE	NAME OF SPONSOR(S) PRESENT	EXPENSES	INCOME	COMMENTS
7/6	JOHN 15	38	FRED + PAM	—	—	2 NEW KIDS, SAM SMITH +

SPECIAL EVENT JOURNAL

EVENT	DATE	AGE GROUP	ATTEND-ANCE	TICKET PRICE	TOTAL INCOME	MONEY SPENT	TOTAL BALANCE	NAME OF SPONSOR(S) PRESENT	COMMENTS
SKATE NITE	9/28	JR. HIGH	28	$3.00	$84.00	$91.00	-6.00	JAN + TERRY	CHARGE MORE NEXT TIME!

- A set of comment cards. Make these available at each meeting. Print them on cardstock.

COMMENT CARD

We invite your comments and requests. Fill out this card and we will contact you as soon as possible. **Please print.**

Name _____

Address _____
STREET _____

CITY _____ STATE ___ ZIP ___ Age ___

Phone _____

Check one or more:

☐ I'd like to become a Christian ☐ I'd like to be on your mailing list
☐ I'd like to receive a Bible or New Testament ☐ I need prayer
☐ I'd like to be baptized ☐ I'd like to become a member of this church

☐ Other: _____

- A contact record sheet, to keep track of the times you meet with individuals.

CONTACT RECORD SHEET

DATE	STUDENT'S NAME	LOCATION	COST	COMMENTS
4·8·85	SAM SMITH, DENNIS OWENS	McDONALD'S	$9.87	NEW COMERS, ATTEND BUENA J.H. INTERESTED IN SPORTS.

- A sign-up sheet to get the names and phone numbers of all the kids who want to be involved in any particular event. Put the sheets on clipboards and pass them around at meetings or hang the clipboards on the wall with hooks. Put appropriate posters by each clipboard so kids will gravitate to the ones that interest them. By the way, use pens instead of pencils for sign up. If a very popular event is limited to a small number of participants, some kids may find that their names have been erased and replaced!

SIGN-UP SHEET

EVENT _____

DATE _____ TIME _____

Your name:	Your phone:
1	
2	

- A mailing address list update card. Mail or hand out this card when you wish to bring your list of names and addresses up-to-date.

ADDRESS UPDATE CARD

We are updating our mail out list. If your name or address on this card is in any way incorrect, please fill out all the lines below.

Name _____

Address _____
STREET

_____
CITY   STATE   ZIP

Phone _____

If you no longer wish to be on our mailing list, we would really appreciate it if you would check the box below and mail this card back to us in an envelope.

☐ Please remove my name from the mailing list.

- A service project sign-up sheet. Hang these forms on clipboards in a conspicuous place, one clipboard for each service activity. One youth minister has about ten of them hanging outside his office, with projects ranging from visiting the orphanage to mowing his front yard! You might try them for church work days, visitation, camp counseling and anything for which you need volunteer help.

VOLUNTARY SERVICE SIGN-UP SHEET

NEED _____

DATE _____ TIME _____

Your name:	Your phone:
1	
2	
3	

- A medical release form. We recommend that you put the signed release forms in a first-aid kit and ALWAYS take them along. It's a good idea to keep photocopies of the originals in a safe place in your office.

MEDICAL RELEASE

Youth's name _____

Address _____

Birthdate _____ Phone _____

Emergency person and phone _____

I (we) understand that, in the event medical treatment is required, every effort will be made to contact me. However, if I cannot be reached, I give my permission to the staff or sponsor to secure the services of a licensed physician to provide the care necessary, including anesthesia, for my child's well-being.

Signed _____ Date _____
(Parent or guardian)

Please list any medical allergies, medications being taken, medical problems, or other pertinent information:

_____
_____
_____

WARNING:

The purpose of a medical release form is stated on the sample above.
Please note that release forms are in no way intended to protect you against any legal action!

- Two blank calendar forms. Fill them out and encourage the kids to hang them up at home.

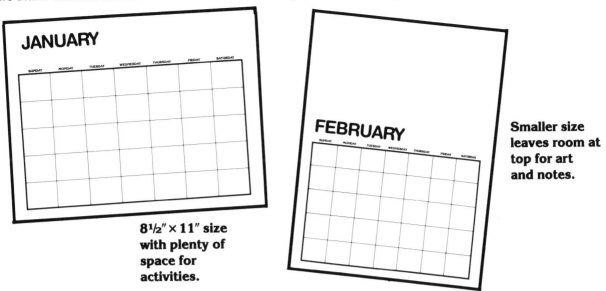

JANUARY

FEBRUARY

8½" × 11" size with plenty of space for activities.

Smaller size leaves room at top for art and notes.

- A "Spiritual Menu" to fill out with your Bible study and deeper life meetings. We've printed two on the page so you can get a lot printed for the money. Or make one for lower grade levels and the other for higher grade levels. Encourage the kids to pass them along to friends who might want to attend.

SPIRITUAL MENU
For Spiritual Appetites
SR. HIGH ———
Sunday 9:30 a.m.
   Bible study, Rm. 22
Sunday 7:00 p.m.
   Bible study and
   Game Nite!
Tuesday 7:00 p.m.
   Deeper Life at
   John's house
Sat. morning 6:30
   Early Bird
      Prayer Breakfast.
JOIN US!

SPIRITUAL MENU
For Spiritual Appetites
JR. HIGH ———
Sunday 9:30 a.m.
   Bible study, Rm. 20
Sunday 7:00
   Wisdom Class.
Wednesday 7:30
   Game Nite and
   Bible study
Sat. morning 6:30
   Early Bird
      Prayer Breakfast.
JOIN US!

- For your students. A Bible study chart and a prayer chart. Helps your deeper kids keep track of their spiritual progress. We think you should give these forms only to kids who want them. Others may be a bit intimidated.

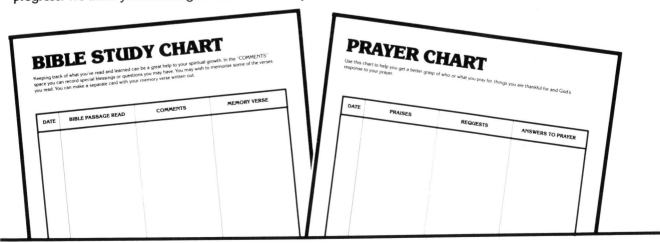

BIBLE STUDY CHART

Keeping track of what you've read and learned can be a great help to your spiritual growth. In the "COMMENTS" space you can record special blessings or questions you may have. You may wish to memorize some of the verses you read. You can make a separate card with your memory verse written out.

DATE	BIBLE PASSAGE READ	COMMENTS	MEMORY VERSE

PRAYER CHART

Use this chart to help you get a better grasp of who or what you pray for, things you are thankful for and God's response to your prayer.

DATE	PRAISES	REQUESTS	ANSWERS TO PRAYER

REGULARLY SCHEDULED MEETING JOURNAL

Name of meeting _____

DATE	SUBJECT OR GUEST	ATTENDANCE	NAME OF SPONSOR(S) PRESENT	EXPENSES	INCOME	COMMENTS

SPECIAL EVENT JOURNAL

EVENT	DATE	AGE GROUP	ATTEND-ANCE	TICKET PRICE	TOTAL INCOME	MONEY SPENT	TOTAL BALANCE	NAME OF SPONSOR(S) PRESENT	COMMENTS

COMMENT CARD

We invite your comments and requests. Fill out this card and we will contact you as soon as possible. **Please print.**

Name _____

Address _____
STREET

_____
CITY   STATE   ZIP

Phone _____ Age _____

Check one or more:

☐ I'd like to become a Christian   ☐ I'd like to be on your mailing list
☐ I'd like to receive a Bible or New Testament   ☐ I need prayer
☐ I'd like to be baptized   ☐ I'd like to become a member of this church

☐ Other: _____

_____

COMMENT CARD

We invite your comments and requests. Fill out this card and we will contact you as soon as possible. **Please print.**

Name _____

Address _____
STREET

_____
CITY   STATE   ZIP

Phone _____ Age _____

Check one or more:

☐ I'd like to become a Christian   ☐ I'd like to be on your mailing list
☐ I'd like to receive a Bible or New Testament   ☐ I need prayer
☐ I'd like to be baptized   ☐ I'd like to become a member of this church

☐ Other: _____

_____

COMMENT CARD

We invite your comments and requests. Fill out this card and we will contact you as soon as possible. **Please print.**

Name _____

Address _____
STREET

_____
CITY   STATE   ZIP

Phone _____ Age _____

Check one or more:

☐ I'd like to become a Christian   ☐ I'd like to be on your mailing list
☐ I'd like to receive a Bible or New Testament   ☐ I need prayer
☐ I'd like to be baptized   ☐ I'd like to become a member of this church

☐ Other: _____

_____

COMMENT CARD

We invite your comments and requests. Fill out this card and we will contact you as soon as possible. **Please print.**

Name _____

Address _____
STREET

_____
CITY   STATE   ZIP

Phone _____ Age _____

Check one or more:

☐ I'd like to become a Christian   ☐ I'd like to be on your mailing list
☐ I'd like to receive a Bible or New Testament   ☐ I need prayer
☐ I'd like to be baptized   ☐ I'd like to become a member of this church

☐ Other: _____

_____

CONTACT RECORD SHEET

DATE	STUDENT'S NAME	LOCATION	COST	COMMENTS

SIGN-UP SHEET

EVENT _____

DATE _____ **TIME** _____

Your name:	Your phone:
1	
2	
3	
4	
5	
6	
7	
8	
9	
10	
11	
12	
13	
14	
15	

ADDRESS UPDATE CARD

We are updating our mail out list. If your name or address on this card is in any way incorrect, please fill out all the lines below.

Name _____

Address _____
STREET

_____
CITY   STATE   ZIP

Phone _____

If you no longer wish to be on our mailing list, we would really appreciate it if you would check the box below and mail this card back to us in an envelope.

☐ Please remove my name from the mailing list.

MEDICAL RELEASE

Youth's name _____

Address _____

Birthdate _____ **Phone** _____

Emergency person and phone _____

I (we) understand that, in the event medical treatment is required, every effort will be made to contact me. However, if I cannot be reached, I give my permission to the staff or sponsor to secure the services of a licensed physician to provide the care necessary, including anesthesia, for my child's well-being.

Signed _____ Date _____
(Parent or guardian)

Please list any medical allergies, medications being taken, medical problems, or other pertinent information:

_____

_____

ADDRESS UPDATE CARD

We are updating our mail out list. If your name or address on this card is in any way incorrect, please fill out all the lines below.

Name _____

Address _____
STREET

_____
CITY   STATE   ZIP

Phone _____

If you no longer wish to be on our mailing list, we would really appreciate it if you would check the box below and mail this card back to us in an envelope.

☐ Please remove my name from the mailing list.

MEDICAL RELEASE

Youth's name _____

Address _____

Birthdate _____ **Phone** _____

Emergency person and phone _____

I (we) understand that, in the event medical treatment is required, every effort will be made to contact me. However, if I cannot be reached, I give my permission to the staff or sponsor to secure the services of a licensed physician to provide the care necessary, including anesthesia, for my child's well-being.

Signed _____ Date _____
(Parent or guardian)

Please list any medical allergies, medications being taken, medical problems, or other pertinent information:

_____

_____

VOLUNTARY SERVICE
SIGN-UP SHEET

NEED _____

DATE _____ **TIME** _____

Your name:	Your phone:
1	
2	
3	
4	
5	
6	
7	
8	
9	
10	
11	
12	
13	
14	
15	

JANUARY FEBRUARY MARCH APRIL MAY JUNE SEPTEMBER JULY OCTOBER AUGUST NOVEMBER DECEMBER

SUNDAY	MONDAY	TUESDAY	WEDNESDAY	THURSDAY	FRIDAY	SATURDAY

SUNDAY	MONDAY	TUESDAY	WEDNESDAY	THURSDAY	FRIDAY	SATURDAY

SPIRITUAL MENU

For Spiritual Appetites

JOIN US!

SPIRITUAL MENU

For Spiritual Appetites

JOIN US!

BIBLE STUDY CHART

Keeping track of what you've read and learned can be a great help to your spiritual growth. In the "COMMENTS" space you can record special blessings or questions you may have. You may wish to memorize some of the verses you read. You can make a separate card with your memory verse written out.

DATE	BIBLE PASSAGE READ	COMMENTS	MEMORY VERSE

PRAYER CHART

Use this chart to help you get a better grasp of who or what you pray for, things you are thankful for and God's response to your prayer.

DATE	PRAISES	REQUESTS	ANSWERS TO PRAYER

SPIRITUAL VITAMINS

Now, here is a section that's really useful! It contains twelve short stories, each with a powerful spiritual point. Include one "Spiritual Vitamin" in each of your major mail outs. At one a month there are enough for a year. You may want to re-write the stories so that they more clearly apply to your particular youth group or situation.

THE MONKEY TRAP

In South America, jungle tribes often earn money by trapping animals. These animals are used for research by scientists the world over.

To trap a monkey, tribe members drill a hole in a coconut, hollow out the insides, and fasten the coconut to a chain.

Deep in the jungle the tribe members locate a band of wild monkeys. As the curious animals cautiously watch from their treetop perches, the tribe members chain the coconut to the base of a tree and make a great show of putting a piece of candy or other bait into the coconut.

After the people leave, it's usually the biggest and dumbest monkey who comes down and sticks his hand into the coconut. But when he grabs the bait, he can't get his fist back out of the hole! Believe it or not, that monkey will hold onto that bait until the natives return, or until he starves to death!

Sin is exactly the same way. It may look good and tasty, like that monkey bait, but it'll put you in chains.

Has a particular sin trap got a hold on you? Don't be a dumb monkey. Let go of that sin and walk away free.

ALEXANDER THE GREAT

A few centuries before Jesus Christ was born, a man named Alexander conquered almost the entire known world using military strength, cleverness and a bit of diplomacy.

A story is told that Alexander and a small company of soldiers approached a strongly fortified walled city. Alexander, standing outside the walls, raised his voice and demanded to see the king. When the king arrived, Alexander insisted that the king surrender the city and it's inhabitants to Alexander and his little band of fighting men.

The king laughed. "Why should we surrender to you? You can't do us any harm!"

But Alexander offered to give the king a demonstration. He ordered his men to line up single file and start marching. He marched them straight toward a sheer cliff.

The townspeople gathered on the wall and watched in shocked silence as, one by one, Alexander's soldiers marched without hesitation right off the cliff to their deaths! After ten soldiers died, Alexander ordered the rest of the men to return to his side.

The townspeople and the king immediately surrendered to Alexander the Great. They realized that if a few men were actually willing to commit suicide at the command of this dynamic leader, then nothing could stop his eventual victory.

Are you willing to be as obedient to the ruler of the universe, Jesus Christ, as those soldiers were to Alexander? Are you as dedicated and committed? Think how much power Christ could have in our area with just a handful of such loyal followers.

JESUS CHRIST THE CORNERSTONE

Thousands of years ago, God promised a man named Abraham that he would be the founding father of a great nation. That promise was fulfilled eventually in the nation Israel.

In order to fulfill His promise, God had to take the land away from the people who lived there, the Canaanites.

The Canaanites were grossly evil people with many incredibly awful practices. For example, they would ritually burn their children in fire as a sacrifice to their false god, Molech.

When a modern-day married couple buys their first home, it's fun to move in and set up house. Many Christian couples dedicate their new house to God with a prayer. But the Canaanites saw things differently. In order to make their new house acceptable to their god, a Canaanite couple would actually kill their firstborn child and set his body on display in the corner of the main room!

When Jesus Christ came to earth, He called Himself a cornerstone, which is to say the key part of a building. (See Matthew 21:42 and Ephesians 2:20-22.)

But perhaps the idea of that firstborn's sacrifice in the corner of the room is part of Christ's thought. Christ gave Himself as a sacrifice for you and me. Let's build our lives on that cornerstone.

THE ORANGE AND THE LEMON

On the outside, lemons and oranges look somewhat the same. But give them a squeeze and one drips sweet juice while the other drips bitterness.

When the pressures of life—the trials, problems, hassles—start to put the squeeze on you, how do you respond?

When a person has a healthy relationship with Jesus Christ, that person will respond to life's pressure the same way Christ would.

Other people will only drip bitterness.

WAX FRUIT

"I am the vine, you are the branches; he who abides in Me, and I in him, he bears much fruit; for apart from Me you can do nothing."

John 15:5, *NASB*

Have you ever seen a little kid walk up to a bowl full of wax or plastic fruit and sink his teeth into a phony banana? Disappointment!

You see, the fake fruit looks good from a distance, but when you get up close you see that it's just a lie. Fake fruit has no real value in itself. Its only purpose is to deceive the onlooker.

The Bible verse above tells us that Christians bear spiritual fruit—things like love, joy, peace in their heart and so on. Like real fruit from a real tree, spiritual fruit has great value! Like the seeds of a genuine apple or orange, spiritual fruit can produce new life, new Christians. And Christians can be good "food." They can nourish each other. Spiritual fruit contains "vitamins" to bring spiritual health to others.

But this real fruit can only be produced by Christians who abide in Christ. All other fruit, no matter how good it looks from a distance, is just a worthless fake.

So stay close to Christ. Like a tree branch which is strongest at the point it's attached to the trunk, you'll be strongest at the point you're closest to Christ.

THE MEAL

What did you have for dinner last night?

Let's say you made a total pig of yourself. You ate, say, six T-bone steaks (rare), fourteen baked potatoes smothered with butter, five quarts of peas with pearl onions and cheese sauce, enough corn on the cob (or is it corn on the cobs? Corns on the cob?) to feed an elephant herd, a bathtub full of salad and . . . well, let's just say that you enjoyed yourself.

If you could possibly eat that much and still manage to stay alive, you might get up (if you could still get up) and go tell your friends about what a fantastic meal you had. You might think and dream about it for days. You might even write a letter to the editor, or call the local news.

But within a short time, no matter how wonderful that meal was, you would begin to grow hungry again. After a few days without food you would be very weak. And in a handful of weeks, you would be starving to death. You would die, scrawny and ugly.

You have to eat food in order to live. Talking and thinking about it just doesn't cut it.

When was the last time you read your Bible or attended one of our Bible studies? The Bible is very much like food. You can't just leave it on the shelf and think about it. You must read it. Often!

POWER

Have you ever turned on a table lamp only to find it doesn't work? You're left in the dark.

So you tap the bulb. Nothing. You shake the lamp a bit harder. Still nothing. But when you put the light bulb into a different table lamp, it works! So there's nothing wrong with the bulb and there's nothing wrong with the electricity.

The lamp itself must be broken. "Hey, I'm no dummy," you say to yourself. "I can fix this."

So you get your folk's tools: Screwdriver, pliers, tape.

"Ha! I'll unplug it so I won't die!" But when you reach for the cord, you find it has been unplugged all the while! Groan.

Everything worked. The bulb was good, the lamp worked fine, and the power was on. But the cord wasn't attached to the source of electricity. No power could flow into the lamp.

There's a lesson to be learned here. You may look good, you may sound fine. But unless you're attached to Almighty God by a relationship with Jesus, you've got absolutely no power for life!

Er—I guess you could be called a dim bulb.

Draw close to God in prayer and Bible study.

SIN AND FORGIVENESS

Have you ever been sitting in science class or watching educational TV and heard the words, "Here's an experiment you can do at home"?

Well, here's an experiment you can do at home!

1. **Fill a glass half-full with pure water.**

2. **Put in two drops of red food color.**

3. **Fill the glass with liquid bleach. Stir. The water will soon turn clear again.**

The red water in the glass represents a person's life, red with sin.

You see, when a sin-filled person comes to Jesus Christ for forgiveness, God's Spirit—like the bleach—completely cleanses us from sin. It's as if that sin was never there! Give God a chance in your life, if you haven't already.

STRANGER AT THE DOOR

It was a snowy Christmas Eve. Inside the warm house, the Christmas tree was cheerfully ablaze with lights and surrounded by dozens of presents.

The man's wife and children were dressed and ready to leave for church. "Come with us," they urged, for they loved him.

"Not me," he snapped. "I don't believe all that religion garbage."

For many years the man's wife had been trying to tell him about Jesus Christ and the salvation He offers. How God's Son had become a human being in order to show us the way to heaven.

"Nonsense," the man always said.

The family left for church and the man was all alone in his cozy country home. He glanced out the window at the cold snowy scene outside. He turned to warm himself by the fire.

But as he turned, his eyes caught a movement in the snow outside. He looked. Cats! Three young cats walking slowly past his window.

"The fools," he thought. "They'll freeze for sure!" The man put on his hat and coat and opened the door. A blast of wintery air sent a shiver through his body.

"Come here, cats! Come inside where there's warmth and food. You'll die out there." But the cats ran away, frightened by the stranger at the door.

He walked outside. "Come back! Don't be afraid, I want to save you."

But the cats were gone. It was too late.

"Well, I did everything I could for them," the man muttered to himself. "What more could I do? I'd have to become a cat myself in order to reach them and save them. If I became a cat, I could tell them and show them. They would have to believe me then, unless they were fools."

Just as he reached the door, the church bells rang in the distance. The man paused for a second and listened. Then he went in by the fire, got down on his knees and wept.

TEMPTATION AND SIN

"No temptation has overtaken you but such as is common to man; and God is faithful, who will not allow you to be tempted beyond what you are able; but with the temptation will provide the way of escape also, that you may be able to endure it."

1 Corinthians 10:13 *NASB*

No temptation is easy to resist—otherwise it wouldn't be a real temptation, would it?

If you are troubled by a certain temptation and are having problems avoiding it, here's a simple story that may be of great help to you:

There were two dogs. The dogs were exactly alike, except that one was black and the other was white. Both dogs were equally strong and fierce.

One day the dogs got into a horrible fight. They struggled and fought. They bit and tore. But because they were exactly alike, neither one seemed able to finish the other off.

Two men came along. One said, "Which dog will win? It's impossible to know!"

The other said, "I know which one will win. I can make either dog win if I so choose."

How could he do it?

The answer is simple. Whichever dog the man chose to feed would eventually win. While that dog would grow strong with nourishment, the other would become weak with hunger.

The same idea applies to your struggle with temptation. If you feed that temptation—by hanging around with the wrong people, for example—the temptation will be too strong to resist. You'll win your battle if you feed the "good" dog.

Pray. Read your Bible. Attend our fellowship. Those are the keys God has given you to help you endure temptation.

RUSSIAN ROULETTE

Have you ever heard of the game, Russian Roulette? A person—a fool!—takes a revolver and loads just one bullet into the cylinder. The fool then spins the cylinder, points the gun at his head and pulls the trigger. If the bullet is not lined up with the firing pin, the person survives. But if the bullet is in firing position, BANG! The player loses.

You would probably agree that the person who plays such a game is a fool.

But I would like to ask you an important question. Have you got your life straightened out with God? If not, sooner or later that bullet will come around. You can thumb your nose at God for only so long.

Don't play with eternity.

THE TELEPHONE

The **TELEPHONE** was invented in 1876 by **ALEXANDER GRAHAM BELL**. The **BELL** telephone is named after him. His assistant was Mister Watson J. Pushbutton. The **PUSHBUTTON** telephone is named after him.

Almost every house in North America has at least one phone. Therefore it is important that we learn to take proper care of our friend the telephone.

EXERCISE is important. Take your phone for walks. Have it do sit-ups. Make calls on it daily. For extra strength and stamina, call **LONG DISTANCE . . .** like **Russia**!

Feed it three times daily. Most phones like cantaloupes. When bathing your telephone, use only warm water in your automatic dish washer. Iron immediately to prevent wrinkles.

Telephones can be taught some great **tricks**, too. With proper coaching your phone can do a double somersault into the pool! Try it. But watch out, telephones are lousy swimmers!

But to really get the most out of your phone . . .

Anytime you have a question, problem or just want to talk, call the special **"Not-so-Hotline!"**

Call our phone #:

Got a question about this month's activities? Want to know more about God? Got problems with something? Give us a buzz.

MISCELLANEOUS CERTIFICATES, AWARDS AND SO ON

What do you give to the girl who made a pig out of herself at the last picnic? How can you find an award suitable for the worst actor in your homemade youth group movie?

Simple! Here's a whole bunch of fun—and some silly—awards for meritorious achievements plus other useful things. Print them on cardstock or special finish papers

National Department of Birthdays

BIRTHDAY CERTIFICATE

ONE HAPPY BIRTHDAY IS HEREBY PROCLAIMED IN HONOR OF

_____

Official Seal of Approval

Presented by the illustrious

_____

Signed _____ Date _____

Cash value of certificate,
one twentieth of one cent.
So we're cheap, so what?

Memory Expert!

"I have hidden your
word in my heart."

Psalm 119:11a, _NIV_

(You may wish to replace this seal with a
gold foil one. You can buy them at any
stationery store.)

Once in awhile it's fun to have a contest where
points are awarded for attendance, bringing friends,
Scripture memorization and the like. Many of the
items in this section can be used as point tokens.

I PIGGED OUT!

DOUBLE DISCOUNT COUPON!

½ price on the next activity!

INSPECTION CERTIFICATE

This premise has been inspected by inspector # _____, and found to be

☐ **A pig sty**
☐ **Slob city**
☐ **Needs improvement**
☐ **Okie-doke**

Signed _____

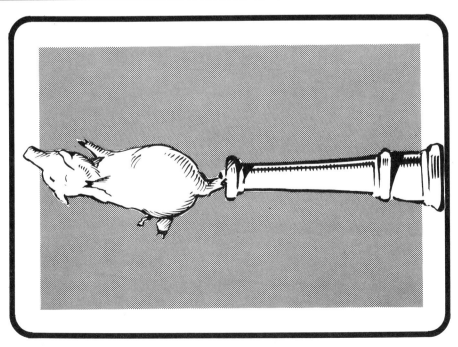

THE IMPERIAL OINKER AWARD FOR MERITORIOUS ACHIEVEMENT!

Awarded to _____

Date _____

ADMIT ONE

Time ——————

Place ——————

Date ——————

ADMIT ONE

Time ——————

Place ——————

Date ——————

'BYE, GUYS!

FREE PASS

Time ——————

Place ——————

Date ——————

Team 2

If you have a weekly game night, you may have experienced difficulty in dividing kids into teams. Instead, hand these badges out at the door. You could print them on peel and stick labels to wear on shirts. After printing them, take a little time to color them in with felt pens.

Team 1

Team 3

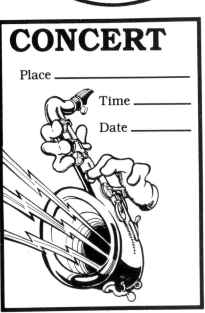

CONCERT

Place ——————

Time ——————

Date ——————

CONCERT

Place ——————

Time ——————

Date ——————

Team 4

HOW TO SURVIVE THE PRINTERS

Nothing is worse than handing over a beautiful paste-up job and getting it back a few days later printed lopsided and in the wrong color!

This section will help you avoid the pitfalls at the printers. Here are some important suggestions:

- Shop around by phone for the best deal.

- Check out what kind of paper is available. If you have a large print run (over a few hundred), the printer may need to order paper, which can add days or weeks to your deadline. Buy the best you can afford, it's always worth it.

- The printing press can never, never improve on what's fed into it. Be sure your pasted-up original is perfect: all the lines straight; clean; no grays (all black); no art peeling off; every date, fact, and figure correct and so on.

- Make clear, concise instructions for the printer. Write your instructions on an attached note or, better still, directly onto a photocopy of the original art.

Sample instructions:

- Write your name and phone number on the back of the original.

- If you have a second color overlay, indicate the color of ink (you'll be asked to pick it from the printer's color samples). Be sure the printer understands exactly how the overlay is to be aligned with the paste-up sheet.

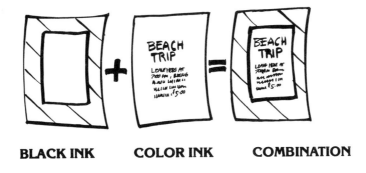

BLACK INK   **COLOR INK**   **COMBINATION**

- You'll need to bring money for a deposit.

SERVICES:

All printers have a piece of paper that lists the helpful services they offer and the cost of each. Pick one up. Here's a typical sample of what you will find:

- Cutting and trimming. The printer can size your printed piece to your specifications. This is a cheap service and worth the price, rather than doing it yourself. But if you have a lot of blank paper that's going to be trimmed off and thrown away, why not print something on it? Design some tickets to the next activity, or write out memory verses. You are paying for the trimmed paper anyway, you may as well use it.

- Folding. Printers have fast and accurate folding machines. Great for getting a big piece of paper into a little envelope. Have you ever tried to tri-fold a thousand mail outs by hand?

Bi-fold   **Tri-fold**   **El-foldo**

- Die cuts. This is very expensive but sometime you may just want to do it. A die is a handmade tool that will punch any shape you specify into a printed product. The perforations on this page are a type of die cut. One youth worker created various shapes of humorous peel and stick labels with a die cut. You can also buy a variety of pre-cut labels, ready to print, peel and stick.

- Screens. In order to print a photograph (something you'll want to do to advertise all the fun things your group does) the photo must be "screened" or broken up into tiny dots. You can have your photos reduced at the same time they are screened so that you can fit several onto one page. Have all your photos screened in one camera shot so that you don't have to pay for each individual photo. By the way, screen your photos BEFORE you glue them to your paste-up. Otherwise the printer might mistakenly screen your whole piece of art. Nothing is worse than having the tiny letters and details broken up into fuzzy dots!

- Special papers. In addition to the cheap bond papers which come in a few standard colors, you can have your product printed on heavy cardstock, special finish papers (such as linen or pebble), super bright colors, peel and stick papers, foils (looks like silver or goldleaf) and who knows what all. See your printer for samples.

- Stats. A printer can photographically enlarge or reduce a piece of art to any size you like. This comes in handy for posters and such.

- Typesetting. Printers do their own typesetting, or they know people who do. If you're lucky enough to have a good one in your area, and have the piles of gold it takes to hire one, you can produce a very nice mail out. You might want to do a "biggie" once a year or so.

GLOSSARY OF ARTIST'S AND PRINTER'S TERMS:

Read over this list and you won't feel as dumb as before!

BLEED: Artwork that extends off the edge of the printed product is said to "bleed." BE SURE your local printer has a printing press that can print a bleed if that's your intention. Many small presses have to have room at the top of the page to grip the paper.

The background bleeds off the printed product.

CAMERA READY ART: This is what you turn in to your printer (besides money). If your original is not camera ready (ready to be put directly on the press) your printer will charge you up to a hundred dollars an hour to fix it for you. When a printer gives a quote to you, he or she will ask you if your art is camera ready, so memorize this one. If you follow all the instructions in this book, your art will be camera ready.

CONTINUOUS TONE PHOTOGRAPH: A black and white photo as it comes from a regular camera is a continuous tone: it contains shades of grey. It cannot be printed on a printing press until it has been "screened." See "SCREEN" below.

COPY: All the words, headlines and subheads on your paper are referred to collectively as the copy. Body copy is the main section of copy other than headlines.

DUMMY: Hey, don't get mad! This is a rough draft version of your final art. Use this for writing notes to the printer.

FLOP: You "flop" an image by photographically making a mirror image like this:

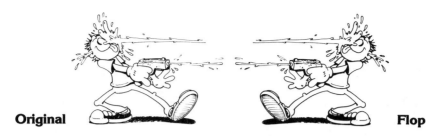

Original   **Flop**

If you want a printer to flop an image, don't use the term "reverse" because that means something entirely different (see below).

FONT: Printed type comes in thousands of different designs known as "fonts." If you have anything typeset, you'll have to pick the various fonts you want.

ABcDEₓGHᵢⱼ

HALFTONE: A halftone is a photograph which has been "screened." (See "SCREENED," below.)

LINE ART: Art that is only pure black and white, no shades of grey. A halftone photograph is in reality line art. Even the most expensive press can only print solid line art. Look closely at that lithograph hanging on your wall and you'll see that each area of it is either a solid color, or fine dots of solid color. Most full-color reproductions are actually printed with only four different colors: black, red, yellow and blue. The tiny dots printed with these colors combine on the page to produce the illusion of full color.

OVERLAY: A layer of art that is intended to be printed as an additional color on the finished product. Many artists use tissue overlays so they can look through the top layer to the art below it as shown here.

Transparent overlay with artwork to complement base art.

Base art

PLATES: This is what the printer actually puts on the press to print your project. They are made photographically from your paste-up. The printer will include a plate-making charge in your bill. If you think you may need an additional print run, see if you can have the plates.

PASTE-UP: This is what you actually produce with all your drawings, lettering and glue.

REDUCTION/ENLARGEMENT: Changing the size of a piece of art, usually expressed in percentages. A 66% reduction will give you a finished product that is ⅔ the size of the original.

 plus 66% reduction equals

You can buy a device known as a "reduction wheel" which will easily and accurately calculate percentages of enlargements and reductions.

REVERSE OR REVERSE OUT: Making a negative image, something a printer can do for you. This is the easy way to put white letters on a black or colored background.

Draw them like this: *Christ the Savior is born —*   Reverse them out like this: *Christ the Savior is born —*

SCREEN: The process by which a printer breaks up a continuous tone photo into tiny black dots so that the printing press can print it. The dots are small and vary in size. The eye sees them as varying shades of gray, the larger dots appearing darker. The number of dots per inch is called the line number. The more dots per inch, the better the printed product will appear. High quality jobs are 250 or more lines per inch. Low quality newspaper photos are less than a hundred. A small print shop can usually deliver about 150 line screens.

Photo screened at 80 lines per inch.

Photo screened at 150 lines per inch.

Extreme enlargement to show detail.

SCREEN DOTS: Large sheets of adhesive backed plastic film with dots printed on them. When stuck to a piece of art and trimmed, they look gray to the eye. The art looks "slicker." They come in various lines per inch (see "SCREEN" above). These and many other patterns are available at good art supply stores.

You might try using some on our clip art. Stay away from extremely fine dots, because they may drop out when printed on a small press or photocopier.

STAT: A high quality photographic reproduction of any art work. If you wish to place two exact images side by side on your paste-up, have a stat made of the original art. Glue the stat down next to the original.

Original

plus stat equals

TRANSFER OR RUB-ON LETTERS: A huge variety of rub-on and peel and stick letters are available at your art supply store. Thumb through the manufacturer's catalogs for ideas.

TYPO (TYPOGRAPHICAL ERROR): We guarantee that, no matter how many times you proofread your finished paste-up, when you take delivery on the expensive printed product the first thing you'll see will be an outrageously obvious mistake!

AND SO . . .

You can see that a piece of camera-ready art can contain many elements: drawings, screened photos, screen dots, an overlay or two, stats that have been flopped or reversed out, headlines and body copy, rub-on letters and more. But don't worry! If you must do all that, just take it one step at a time.

It's better just to keep it simple. We hope we've helped you to do that!

TIPS ON PHOTOCOPYING

If the print shop is too far away, or you don't need the high quality a printing press offers, or if you have only a few dozen copies to make, then you'll want to run your job on a photocopy machine.

Here are a few things to keep in mind.

- You must be careful to eliminate all possible sources of shadows on your original. Shadows are caused by the edges of artwork you've glued to the paste-up, particularly by areas formed as shown.

Shadow will form here.

Carefully trim away overlapping material.

You can prevent shadows by avoiding sharp edges and by flooding correction fluid around the offending areas. Or you can make a photocopy and cover all shadow marks on it with correction fluid for copies, then use it for making the rest of your copies. Also try lightening the exposure control on the copy machine.

- If your church doesn't have an office copier, you should shop around by phone to see who has the lowest photocopier charge (try the Yellow Pages). The lowest price is usually at the print shop, but try the post office, the library, the stationery store and the grocery store.

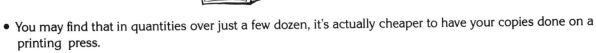

- You may find that in quantities over just a few dozen, it's actually cheaper to have your copies done on a printing press.
- Plain paper copiers are versatile. They allow you to print on both sides of the page, on any color paper and usually in more than one size or odd sizes. Most plain paper copiers can also operate with cardstock. Experiment.
- You can buy overhead projector transparencies to run through plain paper copiers. BE SURE to use the right kind! If a jam happens, ordinary acetate plastic can melt inside a hot copier!
- Cartridge copiers can use several different colors of ink. Multi-color handbills can be produced.

What the future holds:

Laser copiers are on the way. You'll be able to make very high quality black and white and full-color copies from any original art, even color photos. If they can get the price per copy down it could open up some nice possibilities.

TWO GREAT CHRISTIAN CARTOON BOOKS

By *Tom Finley*

Have you ever wished that you could find a good salvation tract that clearly explained the path to new life in Jesus Christ? Presented in a way that any kid would read and truly enjoy it?

Most tracts and Christian comic books either don't appeal to the sort of kids you work with, or they seem too "hellfire and brimstone."

Well, take a look at *DIABOLUS SEEKS REVENGE*

The need for repentance and salvation is clearly laid out in this funny and powerful tale of kings, demons and fools who struggle for control of their world.

"**Junior highers (and their leaders) will enjoy Tom Finley's well-done cartoon *DIABOLUS SEEKS REVENGE . . .*"

—*ETERNITY MAGAZINE*

Your students won't put this book down until they read every exciting page. Each reader will respond to the story's call to continued Bible study and prayer—a growing relationship with Jesus Christ.

WE RECOMMEND THAT YOU . . .

- **Hand out several books as prizes or presents.**

- **Give one to each newcomer. (And get that person's phone number so you can call and see how he or she liked it. Good way to establish a friendship!)**

- **Put a couple in your church library or on your literature table for everyone to enjoy.**

AVAILABLE AT MOST BIBLE BOOKSTORES OR FILL OUT THE ORDER BLANK ON THE NEXT PAGE.

Don't miss these other exciting and helpful YOUTH products from the International Center for Learning:

How to Do Bible Learning Activities Grades 7-12, Book 1, by Ed Stewart and Neal McBride. This book contains over 50 Bible Learning Activities with complete step-by-step instructions and ideas for helping young people discover and apply Bible truths. Discussion activities, research activities, art activities, creative writing activities, drama activities, music activities, puzzles and games are all included in this very helpful manual.

How to Do Bible Learning Activities Grades 7-12, Book 2, by Rick Bundschuh and Annette Parrish. Fifty more new and different Bible Learning Activities with directions and ideas for their use.

Take Me to Your Leader, video tape with E.G. Von Trutzschler. This video training program provides an informative and insightful look at the important subjects of authority and discipline with youth. Includes complete leader instructions and reproducible student guide masters.

Effective Discussions for Youth, video tape. This video training program provides an insight into the importance of question-asking skills in the teaching/learning process. It includes complete leader instructions and reproducible student guide masters.

A Youth Model Lesson, video tape. This video training program shows a youth Sunday School department in action. Practical ways to involve youth in purposeful Bible learning are expertly demonstrated. Special attention is given to small group study, teacher guidance, large group sharing and the creative use of lecture in the teaching/learning process. It includes complete leader instructions and reproducible student guide masters.

For more information on these or other excellent Bible training products for all age groups, contact the International Center for Learning, 2300 Knoll Drive, Ventura, CA 93003, or your local Christian Bookstore.

QUANTITY	ITEM	CODE	PRICE	TOTAL AMOUNT
	HOW TO DO BIBLE LEARNING ACTIVITIES, GRADES 7-12, BOOK I	T3800	$6.95	
	HOW TO DO BIBLE LEARNING ACTIVITIES, GRADES 7-12, BOOK II	T3802	$6.95	
	TAKE ME TO YOUR LEADER VIDEOCASSETTE	T6055	$49.95	
	EFFECTIVE DISCUSSIONS FOR YOUTH VIDEOCASSETTE	T6046	$39.95	
	A YOUTH MODEL LESSON VIDEOCASSETTE	T6044	$39.95	
	DIABOLUS SEEKS REVENGE PAPERBACK	5416704	$3.95	
	WILBUR, MASTER OF THE RATS PAPERBACK	5900059	$3.95	

Take this order blank to your local bookstore or mail it to:

Order Department
GOSPEL LIGHT PUBLICATION
P.O. Box 6309
Oxnard, CA 93031

Tracking code 6011